AF334924

This Recipe Journal Belongs To:

Table of Contents

RECIPE

PAGE

RECIPEPAGE

RECIPE PAGE

RECIPE PAGE

Recipe

RECIPE NAME:

Keto	Low Carb	Paleo	Vegetarian	Vegan	Dairy Free	Gluten Free
☐	☐	☐	☐	☐	☐	☐

QTY	INGREDIENTS	RECIPE DIRECTIONS

NOTES & RECIPE REVIEW

Serves

Prep Time

Cook Time

Tools

Temp

Total	Carbs	Fat	Protein	Cals

Recipe

RECIPE NAME:

Keto ☐ Low Carb ☐ Paleo ☐ Vegetarian ☐ Vegan ☐ Dairy Free ☐ Gluten Free ☐

QTY	INGREDIENTS	RECIPE DIRECTIONS

NOTES & RECIPE REVIEW

Serves	
Prep Time	
Cook Time	
Tools	
Temp	

Total	Carbs	Fat	Protein	Cals

Recipe

RECIPE NAME:

Keto ☐ Low Carb ☐ Paleo ☐ Vegetarian ☐ Vegan ☐ Dairy Free ☐ Gluten Free ☐

QTY	INGREDIENTS	RECIPE DIRECTIONS

NOTES & RECIPE REVIEW

Serves

Prep Time

Cook Time

Tools

Temp

Total	Carbs	Fat	Protein	Cals

RECIPE NAME:

Keto	Low Carb	Paleo	Vegetarian	Vegan	Dairy Free	Gluten Free
☐	☐	☐	☐	☐	☐	☐

QTY	INGREDIENTS	RECIPE DIRECTIONS

NOTES & RECIPE REVIEW

Serves	
Prep Time	
Cook Time	
Tools	
Temp	

Total	Carbs	Fat	Protein	Cals

Recipe

RECIPE NAME:

Keto Low Carb Paleo Vegetarian Vegan Dairy Free Gluten Free

QTY	INGREDIENTS

RECIPE DIRECTIONS

NOTES & RECIPE REVIEW

Serves

Prep Time

Cook Time

Tools

Temp

Total	Carbs	Fat	Protein	Cals

Recipe

RECIPE NAME:

Keto	Low Carb	Paleo	Vegetarian	Vegan	Dairy Free	Gluten Free
☐	☐	☐	☐	☐	☐	☐

QTY	INGREDIENTS	RECIPE DIRECTIONS

NOTES & RECIPE REVIEW

Serves	
Prep Time	
Cook Time	
Tools	
Temp	

Total	Carbs	Fat	Protein	Cals

Recipe

RECIPE NAME:

Keto	Low Carb	Paleo	Vegetarian	Vegan	Dairy Free	Gluten Free
☐	☐	☐	☐	☐	☐	☐

QTY	INGREDIENTS

RECIPE DIRECTIONS

NOTES & RECIPE REVIEW

Serves
Prep Time
Cook Time
Tools
Temp

Total	Carbs	Fat	Protein	Cals

RECIPE NAME:

Keto ☐	Low Carb ☐	Paleo ☐	Vegetarian ☐	Vegan ☐	Dairy Free ☐	Gluten Free ☐

QTY	INGREDIENTS	RECIPE DIRECTIONS

NOTES & RECIPE REVIEW

Serves	
Prep Time	
Cook Time	
Tools	
Temp	

Total	Carbs	Fat	Protein	Cals

Recipe

RECIPE NAME:

Keto	Low Carb	Paleo	Vegetarian	Vegan	Dairy Free	Gluten Free
☐	☐	☐	☐	☐	☐	☐

QTY	INGREDIENTS

RECIPE DIRECTIONS

NOTES & RECIPE REVIEW

Serves	
Prep Time	
Cook Time	
Tools	
Temp	

Total	Carbs	Fat	Protein	Cals

Recipe

RECIPE NAME:

____

Keto ☐ Low Carb ☐ Paleo ☐ Vegetarian ☐ Vegan ☐ Dairy Free ☐ Gluten Free ☐

QTY	INGREDIENTS	RECIPE DIRECTIONS

NOTES & RECIPE REVIEW

Serves	
Prep Time	
Cook Time	
Tools	
Temp	

Total	Carbs	Fat	Protein	Cals

RECIPE NAME:

Keto	Low Carb	Paleo	Vegetarian	Vegan	Dairy Free	Gluten Free
☐	☐	☐	☐	☐	☐	☐

QTY	INGREDIENTS	RECIPE DIRECTIONS

NOTES & RECIPE REVIEW

Serves	
Prep Time	
Cook Time	
Tools	
Temp	

Total	Carbs	Fat	Protein	Cals

Recipe

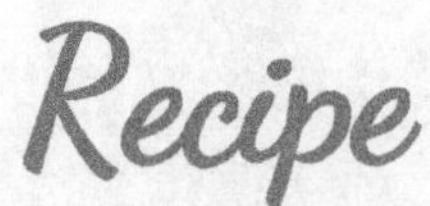

RECIPE NAME:

Keto	Low Carb	Paleo	Vegetarian	Vegan	Dairy Free	Gluten Free
☐	☐	☐	☐	☐	☐	☐

QTY	INGREDIENTS	RECIPE DIRECTIONS

NOTES & RECIPE REVIEW

Serves	
Prep Time	
Cook Time	
Tools	
Temp	

Total	Carbs	Fat	Protein	Cals

RECIPE NAME:

Keto	Low Carb	Paleo	Vegetarian	Vegan	Dairy Free	Gluten Free
☐	☐	☐	☐	☐	☐	☐

QTY	INGREDIENTS	RECIPE DIRECTIONS

NOTES & RECIPE REVIEW

Serves

Prep Time

Cook Time

Tools

Temp

Total	Carbs	Fat	Protein	Cals

RECIPE NAME:

Keto	Low Carb	Paleo	Vegetarian	Vegan	Dairy Free	Gluten Free
☐	☐	☐	☐	☐	☐	☐

QTY	INGREDIENTS	RECIPE DIRECTIONS

NOTES & RECIPE REVIEW

Serves	
Prep Time	
Cook Time	
Tools	
Temp	

Total	Carbs	Fat	Protein	Cals

Recipe

RECIPE NAME:

Keto ☐ Low Carb ☐ Paleo ☐ Vegetarian ☐ Vegan ☐ Dairy Free ☐ Gluten Free ☐

QTY	INGREDIENTS	RECIPE DIRECTIONS

NOTES & RECIPE REVIEW

Serves	
Prep Time	
Cook Time	
Tools	
Temp	

Total	Carbs	Fat	Protein	Cals

RECIPE NAME:

____

Keto	Low Carb	Paleo	Vegetarian	Vegan	Dairy Free	Gluten Free
☐	☐	☐	☐	☐	☐	☐

QTY	INGREDIENTS	RECIPE DIRECTIONS

NOTES & RECIPE REVIEW

Serves	
Prep Time	
Cook Time	
Tools	
Temp	

Total	Carbs	Fat	Protein	Cals

Recipe

RECIPE NAME:

Keto	Low Carb	Paleo	Vegetarian	Vegan	Dairy Free	Gluten Free
☐	☐	☐	☐	☐	☐	☐

QTY	INGREDIENTS	RECIPE DIRECTIONS

NOTES & RECIPE REVIEW

Serves	
Prep Time	
Cook Time	
Tools	
Temp	

Total	Carbs	Fat	Protein	Cals

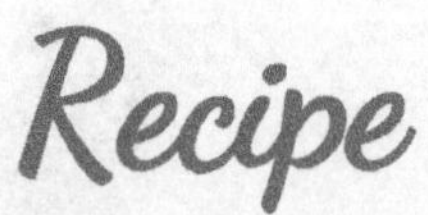

Recipe

RECIPE NAME:

Keto ☐ Low Carb ☐ Paleo ☐ Vegetarian ☐ Vegan ☐ Dairy Free ☐ Gluten Free ☐

QTY	INGREDIENTS	RECIPE DIRECTIONS

NOTES & RECIPE REVIEW

Serves	
Prep Time	
Cook Time	
Tools	
Temp	

Total	Carbs	Fat	Protein	Cals

RECIPE NAME:

Keto	Low Carb	Paleo	Vegetarian	Vegan	Dairy Free	Gluten Free
☐	☐	☐	☐	☐	☐	☐

QTY	INGREDIENTS	RECIPE DIRECTIONS

NOTES & RECIPE REVIEW

Serves	
Prep Time	
Cook Time	
Tools	
Temp	

Total	Carbs	Fat	Protein	Cals

Recipe

RECIPE NAME:

____

Keto	Low Carb	Paleo	Vegetarian	Vegan	Dairy Free	Gluten Free
☐	☐	☐	☐	☐	☐	☐

QTY	INGREDIENTS	RECIPE DIRECTIONS

NOTES & RECIPE REVIEW

Serves	
Prep Time	
Cook Time	
Tools	
Temp	

Total	Carbs	Fat	Protein	Cals

Recipe

RECIPE NAME:

Keto · Low Carb · Paleo · Vegetarian · Vegan · Dairy Free · Gluten Free

QTY	INGREDIENTS	RECIPE DIRECTIONS

NOTES & RECIPE REVIEW

Serves

Prep Time

Cook Time

Tools

Temp

Total	Carbs	Fat	Protein	Cals

Recipe

RECIPE NAME:

____

Keto	Low Carb	Paleo	Vegetarian	Vegan	Dairy Free	Gluten Free
☐	☐	☐	☐	☐	☐	☐

QTY	INGREDIENTS	RECIPE DIRECTIONS

NOTES & RECIPE REVIEW

Serves	
Prep Time	
Cook Time	
Tools	
Temp	

Total	Carbs	Fat	Protein	Cals

RECIPE NAME:

Keto	Low Carb	Paleo	Vegetarian	Vegan	Dairy Free	Gluten Free
☐	☐	☐	☐	☐	☐	☐

QTY	INGREDIENTS	RECIPE DIRECTIONS

NOTES & RECIPE REVIEW

Serves

Prep Time

Cook Time

Tools

Temp

Total	Carbs	Fat	Protein	Cals

Recipe

RECIPE NAME:

Keto ☐ Low Carb ☐ Paleo ☐ Vegetarian ☐ Vegan ☐ Dairy Free ☐ Gluten Free ☐

QTY	INGREDIENTS	RECIPE DIRECTIONS

NOTES & RECIPE REVIEW

Serves	
Prep Time	
Cook Time	
Tools	
Temp	

Total	Carbs	Fat	Protein	Cals

Recipe

RECIPE NAME:

Keto Low Carb Paleo Vegetarian Vegan Dairy Free Gluten Free

QTY	INGREDIENTS	RECIPE DIRECTIONS

NOTES & RECIPE REVIEW

Serves

Prep Time

Cook Time

Tools

Temp

Total	Carbs	Fat	Protein	Cals

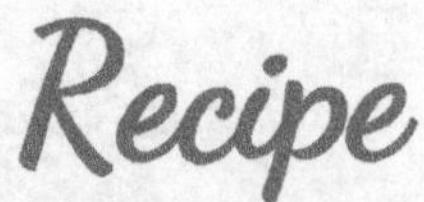

RECIPE NAME:

____

	Keto	Low Carb	Paleo	Vegetarian	Vegan	Dairy Free	Gluten Free
	☐	☐	☐	☐	☐	☐	☐

QTY	INGREDIENTS	RECIPE DIRECTIONS

NOTES & RECIPE REVIEW

Serves	
Prep Time	
Cook Time	
Tools	
Temp	

Total	Carbs	Fat	Protein	Cals

RECIPE NAME:

Keto	Low Carb	Paleo	Vegetarian	Vegan	Dairy Free	Gluten Free
☐	☐	☐	☐	☐	☐	☐

QTY	INGREDIENTS	RECIPE DIRECTIONS

NOTES & RECIPE REVIEW

Serves

Prep Time

Cook Time

Tools

Temp

Total	Carbs	Fat	Protein	Cals

Recipe

RECIPE NAME:

Keto	Low Carb	Paleo	Vegetarian	Vegan	Dairy Free	Gluten Free
☐	☐	☐	☐	☐	☐	☐

QTY	INGREDIENTS	RECIPE DIRECTIONS

NOTES & RECIPE REVIEW

Serves	
Prep Time	
Cook Time	
Tools	
Temp	

Total	Carbs	Fat	Protein	Cals

RECIPE NAME:

Keto	Low Carb	Paleo	Vegetarian	Vegan	Dairy Free	Gluten Free
☐	☐	☐	☐	☐	☐	☐

QTY	INGREDIENTS	RECIPE DIRECTIONS

NOTES & RECIPE REVIEW

Serves	
Prep Time	
Cook Time	
Tools	
Temp	

Total	Carbs	Fat	Protein	Cals

RECIPE NAME:

Keto	Low Carb	Paleo	Vegetarian	Vegan	Dairy Free	Gluten Free
☐	☐	☐	☐	☐	☐	☐

QTY	INGREDIENTS	RECIPE DIRECTIONS

NOTES & RECIPE REVIEW

Serves	
Prep Time	
Cook Time	
Tools	
Temp	

Total	Carbs	Fat	Protein	Cals

RECIPE NAME:

Keto	Low Carb	Paleo	Vegetarian	Vegan	Dairy Free	Gluten Free
☐	☐	☐	☐	☐	☐	☐

QTY	INGREDIENTS	RECIPE DIRECTIONS

NOTES & RECIPE REVIEW

Serves	
Prep Time	
Cook Time	
Tools	
Temp	

Total	Carbs	Fat	Protein	Cals

Recipe

RECIPE NAME:

Keto	Low Carb	Paleo	Vegetarian	Vegan	Dairy Free	Gluten Free
☐	☐	☐	☐	☐	☐	☐

QTY	INGREDIENTS	RECIPE DIRECTIONS

NOTES & RECIPE REVIEW

	Serves
	Prep Time
	Cook Time
	Tools
	Temp

Total	Carbs	Fat	Protein	Cals

Recipe

RECIPE NAME:

Keto Low Carb Paleo Vegetarian Vegan Dairy Free Gluten Free

QTY	INGREDIENTS

RECIPE DIRECTIONS

NOTES & RECIPE REVIEW

Serves

Prep Time

Cook Time

Tools

Temp

Total	Carbs	Fat	Protein	Cals

RECIPE NAME:

Keto	Low Carb	Paleo	Vegetarian	Vegan	Dairy Free	Gluten Free
☐	☐	☐	☐	☐	☐	☐

QTY	INGREDIENTS	RECIPE DIRECTIONS

NOTES & RECIPE REVIEW

Serves	
Prep Time	
Cook Time	
Tools	
Temp	

Total	Carbs	Fat	Protein	Cals

Recipe

RECIPE NAME:

Keto Low Carb Paleo Vegetarian Vegan Dairy Free Gluten Free

QTY	INGREDIENTS	RECIPE DIRECTIONS

NOTES & RECIPE REVIEW

Serves

Prep Time

Cook Time

Tools

Temp

Total	Carbs	Fat	Protein	Cals

Recipe

RECIPE NAME:

Keto ☐ Low Carb ☐ Paleo ☐ Vegetarian ☐ Vegan ☐ Dairy Free ☐ Gluten Free ☐

QTY	INGREDIENTS	RECIPE DIRECTIONS

NOTES & RECIPE REVIEW

Serves	
Prep Time	
Cook Time	
Tools	
Temp	

Total	Carbs	Fat	Protein	Cals

RECIPE NAME:

Keto	Low Carb	Paleo	Vegetarian	Vegan	Dairy Free	Gluten Free
☐	☐	☐	☐	☐	☐	☐

QTY	INGREDIENTS	RECIPE DIRECTIONS

NOTES & RECIPE REVIEW

Serves

Prep Time

Cook Time

Tools

Temp

Total	Carbs	Fat	Protein	Cals

Recipe

RECIPE NAME:

Keto	Low Carb	Paleo	Vegetarian	Vegan	Dairy Free	Gluten Free
☐	☐	☐	☐	☐	☐	☐

QTY	INGREDIENTS	RECIPE DIRECTIONS

NOTES & RECIPE REVIEW

Serves	
Prep Time	
Cook Time	
Tools	
Temp	

Total	Carbs	Fat	Protein	Cals

Recipe

RECIPE NAME:

Keto	Low Carb	Paleo	Vegetarian	Vegan	Dairy Free	Gluten Free
☐	☐	☐	☐	☐	☐	☐

QTY	INGREDIENTS	RECIPE DIRECTIONS

NOTES & RECIPE REVIEW

Serves	
Prep Time	
Cook Time	
Tools	
Temp	

Total	Carbs	Fat	Protein	Cals

Recipe

RECIPE NAME:

Keto	Low Carb	Paleo	Vegetarian	Vegan	Dairy Free	Gluten Free
☐	☐	☐	☐	☐	☐	☐

QTY	INGREDIENTS	RECIPE DIRECTIONS

NOTES & RECIPE REVIEW

Serves	
Prep Time	
Cook Time	
Tools	
Temp	

Total	Carbs	Fat	Protein	Cals

RECIPE NAME:

Keto Low Carb Paleo Vegetarian Vegan Dairy Free Gluten Free

QTY	INGREDIENTS

RECIPE DIRECTIONS

NOTES & RECIPE REVIEW

Serves

Prep Time

Cook Time

Tools

Temp

Total	Carbs	Fat	Protein	Cals

RECIPE NAME:

Keto	Low Carb	Paleo	Vegetarian	Vegan	Dairy Free	Gluten Free
☐	☐	☐	☐	☐	☐	☐

QTY	INGREDIENTS	RECIPE DIRECTIONS

NOTES & RECIPE REVIEW

Serves	
Prep Time	
Cook Time	
Tools	
Temp	

	Carbs	Fat	Protein	Cals
Total				

Recipe

RECIPE NAME:

Keto   Low Carb   Paleo   Vegetarian   Vegan   Dairy Free   Gluten Free

QTY	INGREDIENTS	RECIPE DIRECTIONS

NOTES & RECIPE REVIEW

Serves

Prep Time

Cook Time

Tools

Temp

Total	Carbs	Fat	Protein	Cals

Recipe

RECIPE NAME:

Keto	Low Carb	Paleo	Vegetarian	Vegan	Dairy Free	Gluten Free
☐	☐	☐	☐	☐	☐	☐

QTY	INGREDIENTS

RECIPE DIRECTIONS

NOTES & RECIPE REVIEW

Serves	
Prep Time	
Cook Time	
Tools	
Temp	

Total	Carbs	Fat	Protein	Cals

RECIPE NAME:

Keto	Low Carb	Paleo	Vegetarian	Vegan	Dairy Free	Gluten Free
☐	☐	☐	☐	☐	☐	☐

QTY	INGREDIENTS	RECIPE DIRECTIONS

NOTES & RECIPE REVIEW

Serves

Prep Time

Cook Time

Tools

Temp

Total	Carbs	Fat	Protein	Cals

Recipe

RECIPE NAME:

Keto	Low Carb	Paleo	Vegetarian	Vegan	Dairy Free	Gluten Free
☐	☐	☐	☐	☐	☐	☐

QTY	INGREDIENTS	RECIPE DIRECTIONS

NOTES & RECIPE REVIEW

Serves	
Prep Time	
Cook Time	
Tools	
Temp	

Total	Carbs	Fat	Protein	Cals

Recipe

RECIPE NAME:

Keto	Low Carb	Paleo	Vegetarian	Vegan	Dairy Free	Gluten Free
☐	☐	☐	☐	☐	☐	☐

QTY	INGREDIENTS

RECIPE DIRECTIONS

NOTES & RECIPE REVIEW

Serves	
Prep Time	
Cook Time	
Tools	
Temp	

Total	Carbs	Fat	Protein	Cals

RECIPE NAME:

Keto ☐　Low Carb ☐　Paleo ☐　Vegetarian ☐　Vegan ☐　Dairy Free ☐　Gluten Free ☐

QTY	INGREDIENTS	RECIPE DIRECTIONS

NOTES & RECIPE REVIEW

Serves	
Prep Time	
Cook Time	
Tools	
Temp	

Total	Carbs	Fat	Protein	Cals

RECIPE NAME:

Keto   Low Carb   Paleo   Vegetarian   Vegan   Dairy Free   Gluten Free

QTY	INGREDIENTS	RECIPE DIRECTIONS

NOTES & RECIPE REVIEW

Serves

Prep Time

Cook Time

Tools

Temp

Total	Carbs	Fat	Protein	Cals

Recipe

RECIPE NAME:

____

Keto	Low Carb	Paleo	Vegetarian	Vegan	Dairy Free	Gluten Free
☐	☐	☐	☐	☐	☐	☐

QTY	INGREDIENTS	RECIPE DIRECTIONS

NOTES & RECIPE REVIEW

Serves	
Prep Time	
Cook Time	
Tools	
Temp	

Total	Carbs	Fat	Protein	Cals

RECIPE NAME:

Keto ☐ Low Carb ☐ Paleo ☐ Vegetarian ☐ Vegan ☐ Dairy Free ☐ Gluten Free ☐

QTY	INGREDIENTS

RECIPE DIRECTIONS

NOTES & RECIPE REVIEW

Serves	
Prep Time	
Cook Time	
Tools	
Temp	

Total	Carbs	Fat	Protein	Cals

Recipe

RECIPE NAME:

____

Keto	Low Carb	Paleo	Vegetarian	Vegan	Dairy Free	Gluten Free
☐	☐	☐	☐	☐	☐	☐

QTY	INGREDIENTS	RECIPE DIRECTIONS

NOTES & RECIPE REVIEW

Serves	
Prep Time	
Cook Time	
Tools	
Temp	

Total	Carbs	Fat	Protein	Cals

Recipe

RECIPE NAME:

Keto	Low Carb	Paleo	Vegetarian	Vegan	Dairy Free	Gluten Free
☐	☐	☐	☐	☐	☐	☐

QTY	INGREDIENTS	RECIPE DIRECTIONS

NOTES & RECIPE REVIEW

Serves	
Prep Time	
Cook Time	
Tools	
Temp	

Total	Carbs	Fat	Protein	Cals

Recipe

RECIPE NAME:

Keto	Low Carb	Paleo	Vegetarian	Vegan	Dairy Free	Gluten Free
☐	☐	☐	☐	☐	☐	☐

QTY	INGREDIENTS	RECIPE DIRECTIONS

NOTES & RECIPE REVIEW

Serves	
Prep Time	
Cook Time	
Tools	
Temp	

Total	Carbs	Fat	Protein	Cals

Recipe

RECIPE NAME:

Keto	Low Carb	Paleo	Vegetarian	Vegan	Dairy Free	Gluten Free
☐	☐	☐	☐	☐	☐	☐

QTY	INGREDIENTS	RECIPE DIRECTIONS

NOTES & RECIPE REVIEW

Serves	
Prep Time	
Cook Time	
Tools	
Temp	

Total	Carbs	Fat	Protein	Cals

Recipe

RECIPE NAME:

____

Keto	Low Carb	Paleo	Vegetarian	Vegan	Dairy Free	Gluten Free
☐	☐	☐	☐	☐	☐	☐

QTY	INGREDIENTS

RECIPE DIRECTIONS

NOTES & RECIPE REVIEW

Serves	
Prep Time	
Cook Time	
Tools	
Temp	

Total	Carbs	Fat	Protein	Cals

Recipe

RECIPE NAME:

Keto   Low Carb   Paleo   Vegetarian   Vegan   Dairy Free   Gluten Free

QTY	INGREDIENTS	RECIPE DIRECTIONS

NOTES & RECIPE REVIEW

Serves

Prep Time

Cook Time

Tools

Temp

Total	Carbs	Fat	Protein	Cals

RECIPE NAME:

Keto Low Carb Paleo Vegetarian Vegan Dairy Free Gluten Free

QTY	INGREDIENTS	RECIPE DIRECTIONS

NOTES & RECIPE REVIEW

Serves	
Prep Time	
Cook Time	
Tools	
Temp	

Total	Carbs	Fat	Protein	Cals

Recipe

RECIPE NAME:

Keto | Low Carb | Paleo | Vegetarian | Vegan | Dairy Free | Gluten Free

QTY	INGREDIENTS

RECIPE DIRECTIONS

NOTES & RECIPE REVIEW

Serves	
Prep Time	
Cook Time	
Tools	
Temp	

Total	Carbs	Fat	Protein	Cals

Recipe

RECIPE NAME:

Keto ☐ Low Carb ☐ Paleo ☐ Vegetarian ☐ Vegan ☐ Dairy Free ☐ Gluten Free ☐

QTY	INGREDIENTS	RECIPE DIRECTIONS

NOTES & RECIPE REVIEW

Serves	
Prep Time	
Cook Time	
Tools	
Temp	

Total	Carbs	Fat	Protein	Cals

RECIPE NAME:

Keto Low Carb Paleo Vegetarian Vegan Dairy Free Gluten Free

QTY	INGREDIENTS	RECIPE DIRECTIONS

NOTES & RECIPE REVIEW

Serves

Prep Time

Cook Time

Tools

Temp

Total	Carbs	Fat	Protein	Cals

Recipe

RECIPE NAME:

____

Keto ☐ Low Carb ☐ Paleo ☐ Vegetarian ☐ Vegan ☐ Dairy Free ☐ Gluten Free ☐

QTY	INGREDIENTS	RECIPE DIRECTIONS

NOTES & RECIPE REVIEW

Serves	
Prep Time	
Cook Time	
Tools	
Temp	

Total	Carbs	Fat	Protein	Cals

RECIPE NAME:

Keto	Low Carb	Paleo	Vegetarian	Vegan	Dairy Free	Gluten Free
☐	☐	☐	☐	☐	☐	☐

QTY	INGREDIENTS	RECIPE DIRECTIONS

NOTES & RECIPE REVIEW

Serves
Prep Time
Cook Time
Tools
Temp

Total	Carbs	Fat	Protein	Cals

Recipe

RECIPE NAME:

| Keto | Low Carb | Paleo | Vegetarian | Vegan | Dairy Free | Gluten Free |
| ☐ | ☐ | ☐ | ☐ | ☐ | ☐ | ☐ |

QTY	INGREDIENTS	RECIPE DIRECTIONS

NOTES & RECIPE REVIEW

	Serves	
	Prep Time	
	Cook Time	
	Tools	
	Temp	

Total	Carbs	Fat	Protein	Cals

Recipe

RECIPE NAME:

Keto	Low Carb	Paleo	Vegetarian	Vegan	Dairy Free	Gluten Free
☐	☐	☐	☐	☐	☐	☐

QTY	INGREDIENTS	RECIPE DIRECTIONS

NOTES & RECIPE REVIEW

Serves

Prep Time

Cook Time

Tools

Temp

Total	Carbs	Fat	Protein	Cals

Recipe

RECIPE NAME:

____

Keto	Low Carb	Paleo	Vegetarian	Vegan	Dairy Free	Gluten Free
☐	☐	☐	☐	☐	☐	☐

QTY	INGREDIENTS	RECIPE DIRECTIONS

NOTES & RECIPE REVIEW

	Serves
	Prep Time
	Cook Time
	Tools
	Temp

Total	Carbs	Fat	Protein	Cals

Recipe

RECIPE NAME:

Keto   Low Carb   Paleo   Vegetarian   Vegan   Dairy Free   Gluten Free

QTY	INGREDIENTS	RECIPE DIRECTIONS

NOTES & RECIPE REVIEW

Serves	
Prep Time	
Cook Time	
Tools	
Temp	

Total	Carbs	Fat	Protein	Cals

RECIPE NAME:

____

Keto	Low Carb	Paleo	Vegetarian	Vegan	Dairy Free	Gluten Free
☐	☐	☐	☐	☐	☐	☐

QTY	INGREDIENTS	RECIPE DIRECTIONS

NOTES & RECIPE REVIEW

Serves	
Prep Time	
Cook Time	
Tools	
Temp	

	Carbs	Fat	Protein	Cals
Total				

Recipe

RECIPE NAME:

	Keto	Low Carb	Paleo	Vegetarian	Vegan	Dairy Free	Gluten Free
	☐	☐	☐	☐	☐	☐	☐

QTY	INGREDIENTS	RECIPE DIRECTIONS

NOTES & RECIPE REVIEW

Serves	
Prep Time	
Cook Time	
Tools	
Temp	

Total	Carbs	Fat	Protein	Cals

Recipe

RECIPE NAME:

Keto	Low Carb	Paleo	Vegetarian	Vegan	Dairy Free	Gluten Free
☐	☐	☐	☐	☐	☐	☐

QTY	INGREDIENTS	RECIPE DIRECTIONS

NOTES & RECIPE REVIEW

Serves	
Prep Time	
Cook Time	
Tools	
Temp	

Total	Carbs	Fat	Protein	Cals

Recipe

RECIPE NAME:

Keto | Low Carb | Paleo | Vegetarian | Vegan | Dairy Free | Gluten Free

QTY	INGREDIENTS	RECIPE DIRECTIONS

NOTES & RECIPE REVIEW

Serves

Prep Time

Cook Time

Tools

Temp

Total	Carbs	Fat	Protein	Cals

Recipe

RECIPE NAME:
____

Keto	Low Carb	Paleo	Vegetarian	Vegan	Dairy Free	Gluten Free
☐	☐	☐	☐	☐	☐	☐

QTY	INGREDIENTS	RECIPE DIRECTIONS

NOTES & RECIPE REVIEW

Serves	
Prep Time	
Cook Time	
Tools	
Temp	

Total	Carbs	Fat	Protein	Cals

# Recipe

RECIPE NAME:

Keto	Low Carb	Paleo	Vegetarian	Vegan	Dairy Free	Gluten Free
☐	☐	☐	☐	☐	☐	☐

QTY	INGREDIENTS	RECIPE DIRECTIONS

NOTES & RECIPE REVIEW

	Serves
	Prep Time
	Cook Time
	Tools
	Temp

Total	Carbs	Fat	Protein	Cals

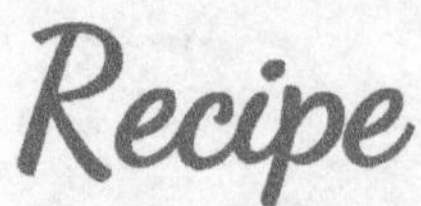

Recipe

RECIPE NAME:

Keto	Low Carb	Paleo	Vegetarian	Vegan	Dairy Free	Gluten Free
☐	☐	☐	☐	☐	☐	☐

QTY	INGREDIENTS	RECIPE DIRECTIONS

NOTES & RECIPE REVIEW

Serves	
Prep Time	
Cook Time	
Tools	
Temp	

Total	Carbs	Fat	Protein	Cals

Recipe

RECIPE NAME:

Keto ☐　Low Carb ☐　Paleo ☐　Vegetarian ☐　Vegan ☐　Dairy Free ☐　Gluten Free ☐

QTY	INGREDIENTS	RECIPE DIRECTIONS

NOTES & RECIPE REVIEW

Serves	
Prep Time	
Cook Time	
Tools	
Temp	

Total	Carbs	Fat	Protein	Cals

Recipe

RECIPE NAME:

____

Keto	Low Carb	Paleo	Vegetarian	Vegan	Dairy Free	Gluten Free
☐	☐	☐	☐	☐	☐	☐

QTY	INGREDIENTS	RECIPE DIRECTIONS

NOTES & RECIPE REVIEW

Serves	
Prep Time	
Cook Time	
Tools	
Temp	

Total	Carbs	Fat	Protein	Cals

RECIPE NAME:

Keto	Low Carb	Paleo	Vegetarian	Vegan	Dairy Free	Gluten Free
☐	☐	☐	☐	☐	☐	☐

QTY	INGREDIENTS	RECIPE DIRECTIONS

NOTES & RECIPE REVIEW

Serves

Prep Time

Cook Time

Tools

Temp

Total	Carbs	Fat	Protein	Cals

Recipe

RECIPE NAME:

Keto	Low Carb	Paleo	Vegetarian	Vegan	Dairy Free	Gluten Free
☐	☐	☐	☐	☐	☐	☐

QTY	INGREDIENTS	RECIPE DIRECTIONS

NOTES & RECIPE REVIEW

Serves	
Prep Time	
Cook Time	
Tools	
Temp	

Total	Carbs	Fat	Protein	Cals

Recipe

RECIPE NAME:

Keto　　Low Carb　　Paleo　　Vegetarian　　Vegan　　Dairy Free　　Gluten Free

QTY	INGREDIENTS

RECIPE DIRECTIONS

NOTES & RECIPE REVIEW

Serves

Prep Time

Cook Time

Tools

Temp

Total	Carbs	Fat	Protein	Cals

RECIPE NAME:

Keto	Low Carb	Paleo	Vegetarian	Vegan	Dairy Free	Gluten Free
☐	☐	☐	☐	☐	☐	☐

QTY	INGREDIENTS	RECIPE DIRECTIONS

NOTES & RECIPE REVIEW

Serves	
Prep Time	
Cook Time	
Tools	
Temp	

Total	Carbs	Fat	Protein	Cals

RECIPE NAME:

Keto Low Carb Paleo Vegetarian Vegan Dairy Free Gluten Free

QTY	INGREDIENTS

RECIPE DIRECTIONS

NOTES & RECIPE REVIEW

Serves

Prep Time

Cook Time

Tools

Temp

Total	Carbs	Fat	Protein	Cals

Recipe

RECIPE NAME:

Keto	Low Carb	Paleo	Vegetarian	Vegan	Dairy Free	Gluten Free
☐	☐	☐	☐	☐	☐	☐

QTY	INGREDIENTS	RECIPE DIRECTIONS

NOTES & RECIPE REVIEW

Serves	
Prep Time	
Cook Time	
Tools	
Temp	

Total	Carbs	Fat	Protein	Cals

Recipe

RECIPE NAME:

Keto	Low Carb	Paleo	Vegetarian	Vegan	Dairy Free	Gluten Free
☐	☐	☐	☐	☐	☐	☐

QTY	INGREDIENTS

RECIPE DIRECTIONS

NOTES & RECIPE REVIEW

Serves	
Prep Time	
Cook Time	
Tools	
Temp	

Total	Carbs	Fat	Protein	Cals

Recipe

RECIPE NAME:

Keto	Low Carb	Paleo	Vegetarian	Vegan	Dairy Free	Gluten Free
☐	☐	☐	☐	☐	☐	☐

QTY	INGREDIENTS	RECIPE DIRECTIONS

NOTES & RECIPE REVIEW

Serves	
Prep Time	
Cook Time	
Tools	
Temp	

Total	Carbs	Fat	Protein	Cals

Recipe

RECIPE NAME:

Keto   Low Carb   Paleo   Vegetarian   Vegan   Dairy Free   Gluten Free

QTY	INGREDIENTS	RECIPE DIRECTIONS

NOTES & RECIPE REVIEW

Serves

Prep Time

Cook Time

Tools

Temp

Total	Carbs	Fat	Protein	Cals

Recipe

RECIPE NAME:

Keto	Low Carb	Paleo	Vegetarian	Vegan	Dairy Free	Gluten Free
☐	☐	☐	☐	☐	☐	☐

QTY	INGREDIENTS

RECIPE DIRECTIONS

NOTES & RECIPE REVIEW

Serves	
Prep Time	
Cook Time	
Tools	
Temp	

Total	Carbs	Fat	Protein	Cals

Recipe

RECIPE NAME:

Keto Low Carb Paleo Vegetarian Vegan Dairy Free Gluten Free

QTY	INGREDIENTS

RECIPE DIRECTIONS

NOTES & RECIPE REVIEW

Serves	
Prep Time	
Cook Time	
Tools	
Temp	

Total	Carbs	Fat	Protein	Cals

RECIPE NAME:

Keto ☐ Low Carb ☐ Paleo ☐ Vegetarian ☐ Vegan ☐ Dairy Free ☐ Gluten Free ☐

QTY	INGREDIENTS	RECIPE DIRECTIONS

NOTES & RECIPE REVIEW

Serves	
Prep Time	
Cook Time	
Tools	
Temp	

Total	Carbs	Fat	Protein	Cals

Recipe

RECIPE NAME:

Keto	Low Carb	Paleo	Vegetarian	Vegan	Dairy Free	Gluten Free
☐	☐	☐	☐	☐	☐	☐

QTY	INGREDIENTS	RECIPE DIRECTIONS

NOTES & RECIPE REVIEW

Serves	
Prep Time	
Cook Time	
Tools	
Temp	

Total	Carbs	Fat	Protein	Cals

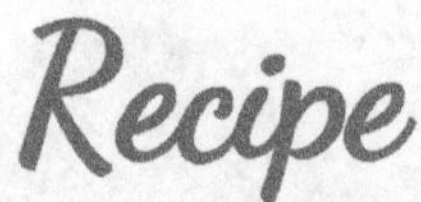

RECIPE NAME:

Keto	Low Carb	Paleo	Vegetarian	Vegan	Dairy Free	Gluten Free
☐	☐	☐	☐	☐	☐	☐

QTY	INGREDIENTS	RECIPE DIRECTIONS

NOTES & RECIPE REVIEW

Serves	
Prep Time	
Cook Time	
Tools	
Temp	

Total	Carbs	Fat	Protein	Cals

RECIPE NAME:

Keto ☐ Low Carb ☐ Paleo ☐ Vegetarian ☐ Vegan ☐ Dairy Free ☐ Gluten Free ☐

QTY	INGREDIENTS	RECIPE DIRECTIONS

NOTES & RECIPE REVIEW

Serves	
Prep Time	
Cook Time	
Tools	
Temp	

Total	Carbs	Fat	Protein	Cals

Recipe

RECIPE NAME:

Keto	Low Carb	Paleo	Vegetarian	Vegan	Dairy Free	Gluten Free
☐	☐	☐	☐	☐	☐	☐

QTY	INGREDIENTS

RECIPE DIRECTIONS

NOTES & RECIPE REVIEW

Serves	
Prep Time	
Cook Time	
Tools	
Temp	

Total	Carbs	Fat	Protein	Cals

Recipe

RECIPE NAME:

Keto   Low Carb   Paleo   Vegetarian   Vegan   Dairy Free   Gluten Free

QTY	INGREDIENTS	RECIPE DIRECTIONS

NOTES & RECIPE REVIEW

Serves

Prep Time

Cook Time

Tools

Temp

Total	Carbs	Fat	Protein	Cals

Recipe

RECIPE NAME:

Keto Low Carb Paleo Vegetarian Vegan Dairy Free Gluten Free

QTY	INGREDIENTS	RECIPE DIRECTIONS

NOTES & RECIPE REVIEW

Serves	
Prep Time	
Cook Time	
Tools	
Temp	

Total	Carbs	Fat	Protein	Cals

Recipe

RECIPE NAME:

Keto | Low Carb | Paleo | Vegetarian | Vegan | Dairy Free | Gluten Free

QTY	INGREDIENTS

RECIPE DIRECTIONS

NOTES & RECIPE REVIEW

Serves
Prep Time
Cook Time
Tools
Temp

Total	Carbs	Fat	Protein	Cals

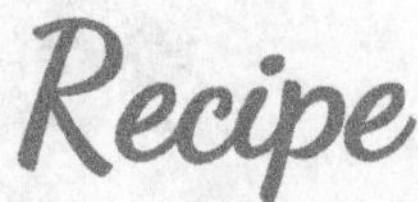

Recipe

RECIPE NAME:

Keto ☐ Low Carb ☐ Paleo ☐ Vegetarian ☐ Vegan ☐ Dairy Free ☐ Gluten Free ☐

QTY	INGREDIENTS	RECIPE DIRECTIONS

NOTES & RECIPE REVIEW

Serves	
Prep Time	
Cook Time	
Tools	
Temp	

Total	Carbs	Fat	Protein	Cals

RECIPE NAME:

Keto   Low Carb   Paleo   Vegetarian   Vegan   Dairy Free   Gluten Free

QTY	INGREDIENTS	RECIPE DIRECTIONS

NOTES & RECIPE REVIEW

Serves

Prep Time

Cook Time

Tools

Temp

Total	Carbs	Fat	Protein	Cals

Recipe

RECIPE NAME:

Keto Low Carb Paleo Vegetarian Vegan Dairy Free Gluten Free

QTY	INGREDIENTS	RECIPE DIRECTIONS

NOTES & RECIPE REVIEW

Serves	
Prep Time	
Cook Time	
Tools	
Temp	

Total	Carbs	Fat	Protein	Cals

RECIPE NAME:

Keto ☐ Low Carb ☐ Paleo ☐ Vegetarian ☐ Vegan ☐ Dairy Free ☐ Gluten Free ☐

QTY	INGREDIENTS	RECIPE DIRECTIONS

NOTES & RECIPE REVIEW

Serves

Prep Time

Cook Time

Tools

Temp

Total	Carbs	Fat	Protein	Cals

Recipe

RECIPE NAME:

Keto	Low Carb	Paleo	Vegetarian	Vegan	Dairy Free	Gluten Free
☐	☐	☐	☐	☐	☐	☐

QTY	INGREDIENTS

RECIPE DIRECTIONS

NOTES & RECIPE REVIEW

Serves	
Prep Time	
Cook Time	
Tools	
Temp	

Total	Carbs	Fat	Protein	Cals

Notes

Notes

Notes

Notes

Notes

Notes